Teacher-Written Student Tests:

A Guide for Planning, Creating, Administering, and Assessing

Patrick W. Miller
Harley E. Erickson

ea PROFESSIONAL LIBRARY
National Education Association
Washington, D.C.

Acknowledgments

The authors wish to thank their wives and their children for their patience, understanding, and support.

Note

The opinions expressed in this publication should not be construed as representing the policy or position of the National Education Association. Materials published as part of the Reference & Resource Series are intended to be discussion documents for teachers who are concerned with specialized interests of the profession.

Library of Congress Cataloging in Publication Data

Miller, Patrick W.
   Teacher-written student tests.

   (Reference & resource series)
   Bibliography: p.
   1. Examinations—Design and construction.
2. Examinations—Interpretation.   3. Grading and
marking (Students)   I. Erickson, Harley E.   II. Title.
III. Series: Reference and resource series.
LB3060.65.M55   1985   371.2'6   85-11582
ISBN 0-8106-1529-0

Contents

Preface.. 5
   Why Should Teachers Test?... 5
   The Purpose of This Book 5

Chapter 1. Planning Classroom Tests.................................... 6
   Instructional Objectives.. 6
   Planning Appropriate Test Items 8

Chapter 2. Guidelines for Developing Classroom Tests 11
   General Guidelines 11
   Specific Guidelines 11

Chapter 3. Assembling and Administering Classroom Tests 17
   Assembling Test Items.. 17
   Preparing Test Directions 17
   Administering Tests 21

Chapter 4. Assessing Test Items... 22
   Item Response Profile.. 22
   Item Difficulty 24
   Item Discrimination 25

Chapter 5. Desirable Characteristics of Tests 29
   Validity... 29
   Reliability.. 31

Appendices
   A. Sample Verbs Used to Identify Specific Student Behaviors.......... 35
   B. Sample Verbs Used in Various Curriculum Areas 36
   C. Sample Test Items 37

Bibliography 64

The Authors

Patrick W. Miller is Associate Professor, Department of Industrial Technology, at the University of Northern Iowa, Cedar Falls. He is the author of *Nonverbal Communication,* published by NEA.

Harley E. Erickson is Professor, Department of Industrial Technology, at the University of Northern Iowa, Cedar Falls.

Preface

WHY SHOULD TEACHERS TEST?

After years of teaching, we have heard numerous complaints from students about tests. These complaints have included such comments as the following:

- The test was not fair.
- The test covered material not found in the instructional unit.
- The test included items with no correct solutions.
- The test was subjective.
- The test items were ambiguous.
- The test was not valid.

The list could easily be expanded; however, it represents the more frequently voiced student complaints. As educators, we must ask ourselves, "Are these complaints warranted?" Although we would like to believe that teacher-made tests are flawless, often they leave much to be desired.

Probably no aspect of education is more talked about and less attended to than student testing. There are several reasons for both the insufficient attention and the poor test construction—time pressures, inadequate test construction skills, and incorrect judgment about students' ability levels.

To ensure effective instruction, teachers need to take into account all aspects of testing. They should consider it not only an evaluation activity, but also a part of the learning process.

THE PURPOSE OF THIS BOOK

All teachers must develop tests to assess student achievements, but creating a test that is valid and reliable is not easy. Tests are not made by haphazardly throwing together test items. Tests that are developed in such a manner provide, at best, vague ideas of student learning. Furthermore, they may well leave students confused, frustrated, and even apprehensive about future examinations.

The development of a good test containing true-false, multiple-choice, matching, or essay items is a laborious and time-consuming task. Although most teachers have received some instruction in test planning, development, and analysis, they do not develop their abilities in these areas until they are faced with the task of designing a test that accurately measures student achievement.

This book offers guidelines, practical suggestions, and examples for developing better teacher-made tests. It is divided into five chapters: (1) Planning Classroom Tests, (2) Guidelines for Developing Classroom Tests, (3) Assembling and Administering Classroom Tests, (4) Assessing Test Items, and (5) Desirable Characteristics of Tests. In addition, Appendix C contains sample test items from various curriculum areas.

The most effective way to use this book is to read it from beginning to end and review the sample test items for the appropriate curriculum area. Although the book is structured sequentially, some readers may choose to skim certain chapters and concentrate on others. In either case, the book should be useful to all middle and secondary school teachers and administrators as well as those preparing to enter the teaching profession.

Chapter 1

Planning Classroom Tests

Classroom teachers should be concerned about assessing student achievement at the end of an instructional unit. The development of a test that accurately measures achievement, however, requires careful planning. This planning includes an examination of student behaviors previously identified in the instructional objectives.

INSTRUCTIONAL OBJECTIVES

Classroom teachers are responsible for writing objectives that describe the terminal behaviors expected of students. Some teachers write objectives with three components: (1) condition, (2) performance, and (3) criterion. Others write objectives that explicitly state only the performance expected of students; they do not include a condition or a criterion.

A condition states important givens or restrictions associated with the setting when the student is exhibiting the terminal behavior.

A performance specifies in terms of observable behavior what the student will be able to do when s/he has demonstrated achievement of the objective.

A criterion (performance standard) describes the level of performance to be considered acceptable.

EXAMPLE 1.1

Objective containing condition, performance, and criterion

Given a plant taxonomy, the student will identify at least five of seven leaves collected during a class field trip.

KEY: _____ = Condition _ _ _ _ = Performance ▬▬▬ = Criterion

EXAMPLE 1.2

Objective with performance only
Solve equations with one unknown.

Objectives can be classified into the three learning domains—cognitive, affective, and psychomotor. In addition, each domain has subdivisions that require increasingly more complex student behaviors.

Cognitive Domain

The cognitive domain (3*) includes the largest proportion of educational objectives. These vary from simple recall of material to synthesizing and evaluating new ideas. The six major subdivisions identified in this domain are knowledge, comprehension, application, analysis, synthesis, and evaluation.

Affective Domain

The affective domain (10) includes student behaviors that emphasize feelings, emotions, attitudes, and values. The five major subdivisions identified in this domain are receiving, responding, valuing, organizing, and characterizing by a value or value complex.

Psychomotor Domain

The psychomotor domain (16) includes student behaviors that emphasize motor skills and activities that require neuromuscular coordination. The seven major subdivisions identified in this domain are perception, set, guided response, mechanism, complex overt response, adaptation, and origination.

Since most instructional objectives are in the cognitive domain, it is imperative that teachers understand the subdivisions (levels) in that domain in order to develop appropriate test items.

Knowledge objectives deal with the student's ability to remember facts, principles, terms, customs, traditions, categories, rules, formulas, procedures, and criteria.

> *Objective*
> Match artists with paintings.

Comprehension objectives require the student to make some elemental use of knowledge—to describe, illustrate, summarize, interpret, note consequences of ideas or methods.

> *Objective*
> Translate Spanish into English.

Application objectives focus on the student's ability to use previously learned material in a setting that is different from the original learning experience—to apply or use ideas, methods, procedures.

> *Objective*
> Calculate the perimeter of a nine-sided figure.

---

*Numbers in parentheses appearing in the text refer to the Bibliography on page 64.

Analysis objectives are concerned with the student's ability to separate ideas into constituent parts in order to note relationships between the parts and the whole.

> **Objective**
>
> Compare the responsibilities of the three governmental branches of the United States.

Synthesis objectives refer to the student's ability to formulate new thoughts from previously learned material.

> **Objective**
>
> Develop a procedure for testing hypotheses.

Evaluation objectives require the student to judge (assess) the value of ideas, methods, or procedures using appropriate criteria.

> **Objective**
>
> Critique two oral speeches presented in class.

Appendix A contains a list of sample verbs used to identify specific student behaviors and Appendix B contains a list of sample verbs used in various curriculum areas. These lists should be helpful to teachers when writing objectives that describe specific observable behaviors in the three learning domains.

PLANNING APPROPRIATE TEST ITEMS

Test items should directly relate to specific behaviors identified by the instructional objectives. The relationship between instructional objectives and assessment procedure cannot be overemphasized.

Test items should be written to reflect the specific domains and levels identified by the objectives. For example, if the objective required the student to synthesize, a test item that required only comprehension would be inappropriate. Synthesizing and comprehending do not require the same behavioral performance; consequently the objective and test item would not correspond. Test items should also assess the student's ability in a particular domain in an appropriate way. For example, if the objective required the student to repair a ten-speed bicycle, a test item that required the student to list the repairs would be inappropriate. Repairing is a psychomotor activity, whereas listing is a cognitive activity at the lowest level.

All secondary curriculum areas place varying degrees of emphasis on instructional objectives in the three domains. Most teacher-written objectives, however, are usually classified in the three lowest levels of the cognitive domain. Attainment of objectives in these levels can be appropriately assessed by true-false, multiple-choice, and matching test items. Objectives in the three highest levels of the cognitive domain are usually assessed by essay test items or more complex choice-type items.

Knowledge test items require recall or recognition of information in substantially the same form as the instruction. Rephrasing, inversion of sentences, and similar form changes do *not* remove a test item from this level.

Comprehension test items require interpretation of a principle in a manner that differs from the instruction, but that implies the principle.

Application test items require use of a previously learned principle in a new setting. These items differ from comprehension items in that they do not imply the required principle. Examples of such items are quantitative problems in mathematics and science.

Higher-level test items in the cognitive domain should require analysis, synthesis, or evaluation of complex situations with appropriate generalizations or inferences.

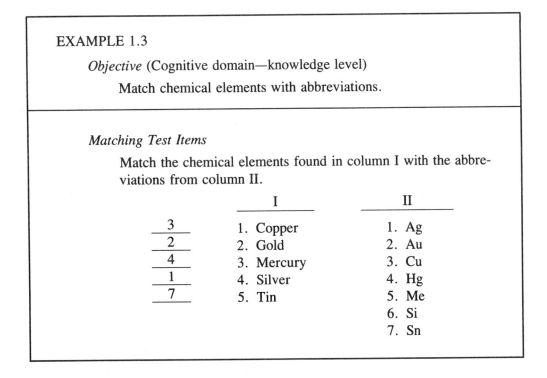

EXAMPLE 1.3

Objective (Cognitive domain—knowledge level)

Match chemical elements with abbreviations.

Matching Test Items

Match the chemical elements found in column I with the abbreviations from column II.

	I	II
3	1. Copper	1. Ag
2	2. Gold	2. Au
4	3. Mercury	3. Cu
1	4. Silver	4. Hg
7	5. Tin	5. Me
		6. Si
		7. Sn

EXAMPLE 1.4

Objective (Cognitive domain—comprehension level)

Identify the dominant tone of a poem.

Multiple-Choice Test Item

The tone of Cummings's poem *Among Crumbling People* is

1. jaunty and bantering.
2. sarcastic.
3. silly.
*4. sorrowful.

EXAMPLE 1.5

Objective (Cognitive domain—application level)

Calculate the area of a circle given the circumference.

Multiple-Choice Test Item

If the circumference of a circle is 44 centimeters, the area in centimeters squared is

   1.   78
*2.   154
   3.   308
   4. 1,078

EXAMPLE 1.6

Objective (Cognitive domain—synthesis level)

Explain how a painting would be different if the artist were alive today.

Essay Test Item

If Leonardo da Vinci had lived at a later time and had painted like the Fauves, how might his painting of the Mona Lisa have been different?

Some expected responses

- He might have flattened the figure somewhat.
- He might have outlined the woman in a dark color.
- He would probably have simplified the background.
- He would probably have placed her in an everyday setting with familiar objects rather than in a mysterious landscape.
- He might have used brighter colors.
- His brush strokes would have been more obvious.
- He would probably have set up some rhythmic pattern in color and line in order to involve the viewer emotionally rather than through the personality of the subject.

The final step in test planning is to determine the appropriate number of test items to write for each level of the cognitive domain. This requires a careful analysis and classification of the instructional objectives. If, for example, the analysis reveals that 50 percent of the objectives are classified as knowledge, then 50 percent of the test items should assess recall of the facts, principles, and laws taught in the instructional unit. If the analysis indicates that the remaining objectives are classified as 25 percent comprehension, 15 percent application, and 10 percent higher levels, then appropriate test items should be written to reflect this instructional emphasis.

Chapter 2

Guidelines for Developing Classroom Tests

The most frequently used teacher-made tests to assess student achievement are true-false, multiple choice, matching, and essay. Each of these tests has distinct advantages and disadvantages. True-false, multiple-choice, and matching tests are relatively easy to write, they sample a large amount of content, and they are quickly and objectively scored. However, these tests are frequently limited to facts, they encourage guessing, and they usually do not measure higher levels of learning (analysis, synthesis, and evaluation). The major advantage of the essay test is that it requires students to demonstrate attainment of instructional objectives in the higher levels of the cognitive domain. In addition, it allows students to express themselves in their own words. Its major disadvantage is the subjectivity associated with rating student responses.

There are several general and specific guidelines that teachers should apply when writing any type of classroom test.

GENERAL GUIDELINES

The general guidelines for developing classroom tests include the following:

- Test items should be directly related to the instructional objectives.
- Test items should be clear and free from ambiguities.
- Test items should use vocabulary appropriate to the educational level of the students.
- Test items should be grammatically correct and free from spelling and typing errors.
- Test items should be realistic and practical; that is, they should call for information that students must use.
- One test item should not be based upon the response to another, nor should it provide a clue to other items.
- Test items should minimize or avoid the use of textbook or stereotyped language.
- Test items should cite authorities for statements that might be considered debatable or based on opinion.
- Test items should avoid needlessly complex sentences.
- Test items should use the simplest method for recording a response.
- Test directions should be clear and complete.

SPECIFIC GUIDELINES

In addition to general guidelines, specific guidelines should be used in developing true-false, multiple-choice, matching, and essay test items. These guidelines, coupled with examples, are designed to provide teachers with a sense of direction for constructing appropriate test items.

11

True-False Items

The true-false test consists of statements that are either true or false. The student must read the statements and choose one of two alternatives: true or false, yes or no, right or wrong, or plus or minus (+ or –). The following are guidelines for constructing true-false test items:

● Each test item should focus on a single important idea.
● A test item should be false because it contains an important concept that is incorrect, not because it contains an insignificant error.
● Each test item should be written as an affirmative rather than a negative statement.

EXAMPLE 2.1

| Poor | T | F | James Madison was not a President of the United States. |
| Good | T | F | James Madison was a President of the United States. |

● Test items should never use double negatives.

EXAMPLE 2.2

| Poor | T | F | Watergate was not an instance of unauthorized entry. |
| Good | T | F | Watergate was an instance of unauthorized entry. |

● Test items should be brief, but not at the expense of clarity. Avoid sentences in excess of 20 words because they can be guessed true more often than false. A lengthy statement containing dependent clauses and phrases reduces the probability that an item is false.
● Test items containing specific citations or enumerations should be used with caution. Such statements are more likely to be true than false.
● Test items should not use specific determiners, such as *all, always, exactly, never, totally, entirely, completely, solely, fully, absolutely, exclusively, only, none, nothing,* and *alone,* because they are likely to be false.
● Test items should be true or false without qualification. Statements containing qualifiers, such as *sometimes, maybe, often, several, as a rule, should, may, most, some,* and *generally,* are more likely to be true than false.
● Test items that are true should not be consistently longer than those that are false.
● Tests should consist of approximately equal numbers of true and false statements.

EXAMPLE 2.3

Sample True-False Items

   F   1. X = 8 in the equation $3X + 6 = 18$.

   T   2. The area of a rectangle 5 cm wide × 8 cm long is 40 cm².

Multiple-Choice Items

Each item in a multiple-choice test consists of a stem and alternatives (correct response and several distractors). The stem presents a statement or question; the correct response provides a solution or answer. The distractors are incorrect choices that should attract students who have not mastered the material, yet they should not confuse students who have attained mastery.

There are several guidelines for writing stems and alternatives.

Rules for Developing Stems

The rules for developing stems of multiple-choice items include the following:

- Stems should be stated as briefly and concisely as possible.
- Stems should be concerned with only one central problem.
- Stems should be direct questions or incomplete statements.
- Stems should be stated positively.
- Stems should include as much of the item as possible so that students need not reread the same material in each alternative.

EXAMPLE 2.4

Poor   If a gas is compressed

                *1. its temperature increases.
                 2. its temperature decreases.
                 3. its temperature remains the same.
                 4. its temperature sometimes increases and sometimes decreases.

Good   Compressing a gas causes its temperature to

                *1. increase.
                 2. decrease.
                 3. remain the same.
                 4. fluctuate between increase and decrease.

- Stems should not use "a" or "an" as the final word if it serves as a clue to the correct response.

EXAMPLE 2.5

Poor	Oak is a material that is an
	*1. open grain wood.
	2. closed grain wood.
	3. soft wood.
	4. masonite.
Good	Oak is a material that is a/an
	*1. open grain wood.
	2. closed grain wood.
	3. soft wood.
	4. masonite.

Rules for Developing Alternatives

Multiple-choice item alternatives consist of three or four distractors (incorrect choices) and the correct response. The rules for developing these alternatives include the following:

- Alternatives must include one choice that is clearly the best (the correct response); the remaining alternatives should appear plausible to the uninformed or partially informed student. An alternative should not be included solely for the purpose of humor.
- Alternatives should be grammatically correct and consistent with the stem.
- Alternatives should include the statements "none of the above" or "all of the above" with caution.
- Alternatives should use the appropriate punctuation marks.
- Alternatives for each test item should be approximately equal in length.
- Alternatives should be arranged so that the correct responses for all multiple-choice items occur in a random order.
- Alternatives should be as brief as possible.
- The format of the test should be consistent.

EXAMPLE: 2.6

Sample Multiple-Choice Items

1. The measure of central tendency computed when it is desired to avoid the effect of extreme scores is the
   1. mean.
   *2. median.
   3. mode.
   4. variance.

2. The probability of observing two heads and one tail in a single toss of three coins is
   1. 1/8.
   2. 2/8.
   *3. 3/8.
   4. 5/8.

14

Matching Items

There are times when matching test items are the most appropriate for assessing student achievement in an instructional unit. Matching tests require students to respond by pairing statements or words in two columns of related material. The typical matching exercise consists of a list of statements in column I (primary column) and a list of responses in column II (response column).

Specific rules for developing matching test items include the following:

- Directions should clearly describe the contents of columns I and II and the basis for matching.
- Matching exercises should consist of homogeneous material (for example, historical events and dates).
- The entire matching exercise should be on the same page.
- Responses in column II should be arranged in some systematic manner: alphabetically, chronologically, or, in the case of numerical responses, in ascending or descending order.
- Column II should contain only one correct match for each statement in column I.
- The statements in column I should be longer than the responses in column II because the statements should serve as stems and the responses as alternatives. This provides a more efficient visual arrangement for the student.

EXAMPLE 2.7

Sample Matching Items

Directions: Match the inventions found in column I with the inventors in column II.

	I	II
3	Atlantic cable	1. Colt
9	cotton gin	2. Edison
6	electric starter	3. Field
5	sewing machine	4. Franklin
8	steam engine	5. Howe
7	wireless telegraphy	6. Kettering
		7. Marconi
		8. Watt
		9. Whitney

Essay Items

Essay test items usually consist of questions that require the student to demonstrate attainment of instructional objectives in the higher levels of the cognitive domain. Responses should indicate the student's ability to organize facts and ideas in a clear and meaningful way.

A helpful resource for teachers preparing essay test items is *Writing in the Content Areas: Senior High School* by Tchudi and Yates (19, pp. 70-73). Emphasizing the relation between written expression and understanding of content, these authors recommend designing essay examinations that make it easier for students to produce good writing as well as to "display their content knowledge as fully and clearly as they are able" (19, p. 70). To accomplish this, they suggest giving students several options—a dialogue, a story, an on-the-scene report, an interview, a scenario—rather than confining them to an essay to answer such examination questions. According to Tchudi and Yates, most content knowledge can be expressed clearly and fully in different ways.

To help students organize their facts and ideas, especially when time is limited, teachers can remind students to apply what they know about the writing process to the examination. For example, they should divide their available time into three parts: "a brief time for prewriting [thinking and planning], a longer time for writing, and a short time for revision and copyediting" (19, p. 72). Tchudi and Yates also offer specific strategies for each part of the writing process (19, pp. 72-73).

Several rules for developing essay questions are as follows:

- Indicate a limit (space, words, time) for each item.
- State items clearly and identify specifically what the student is to accomplish.
- Develop a sample answer (before administering the test) that indicates the main points expected in the response.

EXAMPLE 2.8

Sample Essay Item

During this class period, write an essay in which you state and explain your position on the issue of capital punishment. In explaining your position be sure to consider both sides of the issue, and critique arguments you consider irrelevant and/or indefensible.

Points for Grading

Pro Arguments:
● Society must protect itself against violent criminals.	5
● Society must establish deterrents to crime.	5
● Death is a just punishment.	5

Con Arguments:
● Death penalties are unjust.	5
● Execution is not a morally defensible response to crime.	5
● Capital punishment does not deter crime.	5

● Two individual counters and/or critiques to relevant pro/con arguments.	10
● Individual's position	10
Total	50

Chapter 3

Assembling and Administering Classroom Tests

After carefully preparing test items, teachers need to give similar attention to assembling the items, writing the directions, and administering the test. Inattention to these factors may adversely affect the test results.

ASSEMBLING TEST ITEMS

To create better tests, teachers need to (1) review instructional objectives, (2) select or write items that assess these objectives, and (3) properly arrange the items in a final test form.

To improve existing tests, teachers should review the items rewriting those that (1) are unclear, (2) have poor (implausible) distractors, (3) are too easy, (4) are too difficult, and (5) have technical and/or grammatical errors. One way to go about this process is to ask a colleague to review the test and supply information about individual items as well as the test as a whole. Teachers who use this "teacher review method" can obtain information about item ambiguity and other flaws that may have gone unnoticed.

There are several guidelines to follow when assembling test items:

- Arrange items by type (all matching together, etc.).
- Arrange items according to instructional content.
- Arrange items in order of increasing difficulty. This may help relieve test anxiety and enable students to proceed in a timely manner to later items.

PREPARING TEST DIRECTIONS

A good test includes directions that explain how to respond to the item(s). Poorly written directions often mislead and confuse students. Directions should state clearly and concisely what, how, where, and when students should answer. Some tests (true-false and multiple choice, for example) require simple directions; others (matching and essay) may require more complex directions.

Whenever possible, it is highly recommended that teachers provide a sample for each type of test item.

EXAMPLE 3.1

Directions: Circle the number of the best answer to each question.

Sample	How many days are in a week?
	1. 3
	2. 5
	3. 6
	④ 7

1. How many centimeters in 1 meter?

    1.   10
    2.   12
   ③   100
    4. 1000

2. How many millimeters in 1 meter?

    1.   10
    2.   12
    3.   100
   ④ 1000

Sample directions for use with true-false, multiple-choice, and matching test items for both answer sheet and test booklet responses follow.

True-False Directions

Answer Sheet: Below are a number of statements; some are true and some are false. If a statement is true, darken the first space on the answer sheet that corresponds to the item number with a #2 pencil. If the item is false, darken the second space on the answer sheet that corresponds to the item number.

EXAMPLE 3.2

    1.   Copper is a conductor of heat and electricity.

Answer Sheet

	T	F			
1.	1	2	3	4	5
	▬	═══	═══	═══	═══

Test Booklet: Below are a number of statements; some are true and some are false. If the statement is true, write T in the blank preceding the item number. If the item is false, write F in the blank preceding the item number.

Multiple-Choice Directions

Answer Sheet: Below are a number of items, each followed by four alternatives, only one of which is correct. Indicate your selection of the alternative that correctly completes the item or answers the question by darkening the space below the corresponding number on the answer sheet with a *#2* pencil.

```
┌─────────────────────────────────────────────────────────────────┐
│                                                                   │
│    EXAMPLE 3.4                                                    │
│                                                                   │
│       2.  The ability to do work or perform some action is        │
│               1.  energy.                                         │
│               2.  kilowatts.                                      │
│               3.  power.                                          │
│               4.  wave motion.                                    │
│                                                                   │
│    Answer Sheet                                                   │
│                                                                   │
│    2.      1      2      3      4      5                           │
│          ███    ═══    ═══    ═══    ═══                          │
│                                                                   │
└─────────────────────────────────────────────────────────────────┘
```

Test Booklet: Below are a number of items, each followed by four alternatives, only one of which is correct. Indicate your selection of the alternative that correctly completes the item or answers the question by placing the corresponding number in the blank to the left of the item number.

```
┌─────────────────────────────────────────────────────────────────┐
│                                                                   │
│    EXAMPLE 3.5                                                    │
│                                                                   │
│    ___1___      2.  The ability to do work or perform some action is│
│                        1.  energy.                                │
│                        2.  kilowatts.                             │
│                        3.  power.                                 │
│                        4.  wave motion.                           │
│                                                                   │
└─────────────────────────────────────────────────────────────────┘
```

Matching Directions

Answer Sheet: Below are two columns. Column I describes four measurement instruments. Column II lists five types of tests or inventories. Match each description in column I with the test or inventory in column II by darkening the space below the corresponding number on the answer sheet with a *#2* pencil.

EXAMPLE 3.6

I	II
3. Provides a measure of personal likes and dislikes.	1. Achievement test
4. Measures potential ability or capacity to learn various skills and acquire new knowledge.	2. Aptitude test
5. Measures amount of knowledge or skills child has acquired in particular subject field.	3. Attitude measure
6. Measures global capacity to act purposefully, think logically, and deal with environment.	4. General mental ability test
	5. Interest inventory

Answer Sheet

	1	2	3	4	5
3.	===	===	■■■	===	===
4.	===	■■■	===	===	===
5.	■■■	===	===	===	===
6.	===	===	===	■■■	===

Test Booklet: Below are two columns. Column I describes four measurement instruments. Column II lists five types of tests or inventories. Match each description in column I with the test or inventory in column II by placing the appropriate number in the blank to the left of the item number.

EXAMPLE 3.7

	I	II
3	3. Provides a measure of personal likes and dislikes.	1. Achievement test
2	4. Measures potential ability or capacity to learn various skills and acquire new knowledge.	2. Aptitude test
1	5. Measures amount of knowledge or skills child has acquired in particular subject field.	3. Attitude measure
4	6. Measures global capacity to act purposefully, think logically, and deal with environment.	4. General mental ability test
		5. Interest inventory

ADMINISTERING TESTS

When administering tests, teachers must provide all students with the opportunity to demonstrate attainment of the instructional objectives. Therefore, a careful consideration of the physical setting and the psychological factors that may affect students' test results is important.

Physical Setting

Since most tests are administered in classrooms, teachers should attempt to provide an atmosphere conducive to successful test taking. Ideal testing conditions include the following:

- Ample student space.
- Proper lighting and ventilation.
- Comfortable temperature and reasonable air circulation.

Some classroom conditions are beyond the teacher's control; others, however, can be modified by a sensitive teacher. For example, if the afternoon sun is creating a glare for certain students, adjusting the window covering could eliminate the problem. The point is that teacher sensitivity to students' reactions can improve the physical setting.

Teachers also need to be attentive to distractions from hallways, adjacent rooms, or outside the building. Although they cannot anticipate many of these distractions, they can avoid most of them by carefully selecting the best time to administer the test.

Psychological Conditions

The psychological atmosphere associated with testing is often overlooked even though these factors can affect test results as much as, if not more than, the physical conditions. If students feel tense, overanxious, or pressured, their performance during testing may be hindered. Teachers need to be especially alert to these factors so that testing situations may facilitate accurate assessments.

Teachers can create a positive testing atmosphere by explaining the reason for the test and adequately preparing students. They can best accomplish this by reviewing the instructional content to be covered by the test and providing students with sample test items. The nature of the test and the amount of time students need for preparation will dictate the best time for this orientation. It may be a week or more before the test, or it may be immediately before the test. Keep in mind, however, that even with careful preparation, some students will still be apprehensive because of the evaluative nature of testing.

Chapter 4

Assessing Test Items

After scoring and returning a test, most teachers allow time for students to ask questions about specific items. This procedure provides the teacher with feedback about the entire test (directions, items, and scoring procedures) and can also identify items that are ambiguous or otherwise flawed. Unfortunately, this informal feedback is often the only analysis teachers make before administering the test again. The entire test can be more systematically appraised by using three techniques: analyzing an item response profile, calculating item difficulty, and determining item discrimination.

ITEM RESPONSE PROFILE

Determining the appropriateness or effectiveness of each test item requires an analysis of student responses. An item response profile can provide information about the characteristics of each item and it is particularly valuable in identifying distractors used in multiple-choice items that may need revision.

Suppose a class recently completed a test, and in addition to student feedback, the teacher desires more detailed information about each item. Examples 4.1 through 4.3 provide sample test items and response profiles for a class of 25 students. These examples illustrate the use of this technique to determine how well each alternative functions in a multiple-choice item.

EXAMPLE 4.1

Test Item

If the odds in favor of an event occurring are 6 to 1, the probability of this event occurring is

    1. 1/7
    2. 1/6
 *3. 6/7
    4. 1/13

Response Profile

1	2	*3	4	(Alternatives)
4	6	15	0	(# of student responses)

The response profile for the item in Example 4.1 shows that no students responded to alternative 4. This should immediately indicate to the teacher that alternative 4 needs revision if the item is to be retained with four choices.

22

```
┌─────────────────────────────────────────────────────────────────┐
│                                                                   │
│   EXAMPLE 4.2                                                     │
│                                                                   │
│   Test Item                                                       │
│                                                                   │
│         On a true-false test of N items, the test score (A) is    │
│         computed as the number right (R) minus the number         │
│         wrong (W). If Joe responds to all the items and R are      │
│         right, what score is record-ed for Joe? (A, N, R)         │
│                                                                   │
│              *1.  A = 2R – N                                      │
│               2.  A = R – (R – N)                                 │
│               3.  A = R/N                                         │
│               4.  A = R – N                                       │
│                                                                   │
├─────────────────────────────────────────────────────────────────┤
│                                                                   │
│   Response Profile                                                │
│              *1    2    3    4      (Alternatives)                │
│               8    5    6    6      (# of student responses)      │
│                                                                   │
└─────────────────────────────────────────────────────────────────┘
```

The response profile for the item in Example 4.2 indicates that the item is faulty since almost equal numbers of students responded to the correct answer and the three distractors. This item should be examined for complexity as well as for an appropriate relationship to the instructional objective(s).

```
┌─────────────────────────────────────────────────────────────────┐
│                                                                   │
│   EXAMPLE 4.3                                                     │
│                                                                   │
│   Test Item                                                       │
│                                                                   │
│         If you are involved in an automobile accident and an      │
│         injury oc-curs, the first place you should call is        │
│                                                                   │
│               1.  the police station.                            │
│              *2.  a hospital.                                     │
│               3.  the insurance company.                         │
│               4.  your home.                                      │
│                                                                   │
├─────────────────────────────────────────────────────────────────┤
│                                                                   │
│   Response Profile                                                │
│               1   *2    3    4      (Alternatives)                │
│              12    8    3    2      (# of student responses)      │
│                                                                   │
└─────────────────────────────────────────────────────────────────┘
```

Distractor 1 in Example 4.3 should be carefully examined, since more students responded to it than to the keyed (*) alternative.

ITEM DIFFICULTY

Item difficulty (sometimes referred to as an easiness index) indicates the proportion of students who responded correctly to a test item. The difficulty of an item can be expressed on a scale from 0.00 to 1.00. A value of 0.00 indicates that no students responded correctly to the item; a value of 1.00 indicates that all students responded correctly. For example, a difficulty index of .70 indicates that 70 percent of the students responded correctly to a particular item.

The difficulty of an item is calculated by the following formula:

FORMULA

$$\text{Item difficulty} = \frac{\text{\# of students responding correctly}}{\text{\# of students in the class}}$$

Examples 4.4 and 4.5 provide sample test items with a response profile and an item difficulty calculation for a class of 25 students.

EXAMPLE 4.4

Test Item

The design principle that stresses the quality of equilibrium is

    *1. balance.
    2. proportion.
    3. unity.
    4. variety.

Response Profile

*1	2	3	4	(Alternatives)
18	3	2	2	(# of student responses)

Item Difficulty

$$\text{Item difficulty} = \frac{18}{25} = .72$$

Example 4.4 identifies a relatively easy item, since 72 percent of the students responded correctly. The item difficulty of .72 signifies that approximately three-fourths of the class has demonstrated attainment of the instructional objective assessed by the item.

```
┌──────────────────────────────────────────────────────────────────────┐
│  EXAMPLE 4.5                                                           │
│                                                                        │
│     Test Item                                                          │
│                                                                        │
│        A symbol in poetry                                              │
│              *1.  stands for something else.                           │
│               2.  is a simile or metaphor.                             │
│               3.  is easy to understand.                               │
│               4.  appeals to the ear.                                  │
├──────────────────────────────────────────────────────────────────────┤
│     Response Profile                                                   │
│              *1     2      3      4       (Alternatives)               │
│               8     5      6      6       (# of student responses)     │
├──────────────────────────────────────────────────────────────────────┤
│     Item Difficulty                                                    │
│                                      8                                 │
│              Item difficulty  =  ─────  =  .32                         │
│                                     25                                 │
└──────────────────────────────────────────────────────────────────────┘
```

Example 4.5 shows an item difficulty of .32, indicating a difficult item. According to the response profile, students responded randomly; thus the item has serious faults. Ideally, a test should seldom contain items with difficulties below .30.

ITEM DISCRIMINATION

In addition to assessing a test by analyzing the item response profile and calculating the item difficulty, teachers can determine if a test item distinguishes between highest- and lowest-scoring students. This measure is called item discrimination.

The procedure for determining item discrimination involves the following steps:

- Arrange test scores in order from highest to lowest.
- Determine the number of students for 25 percent of the class (K).
- Identify the highest 25 percent and the lowest 25 percent of the scores.
- Determine the number of students from the highest 25 percent who responded correctly to the test item (H).
- Determine the number of students from the lowest 25 percent who responded correctly to the test item (L).

Test items can have positive, negative, or no discrimination, expressed on a scale from −1.00 to +1.00. Item discrimination is calculated by the following formula:

```
┌──────────────────────────────────────────────────────────────────────┐
│  FORMULA                                                              │
│                                      H − L                            │
│       Item discrimination  =  ───────────                             │
│                                        K                              │
│                                                                        │
│        H = # of highest-scoring students responding correctly to the item │
│        L = # of lowest-scoring students responding correctly to the item  │
│        K = # of students for 25% of the class                        │
└──────────────────────────────────────────────────────────────────────┘
```

An item discriminates positively if more highest-scoring than lowest-scoring students respond correctly. Maximum positive discrimination occurs when all highest-scoring students respond correctly to the item and no lowest-scoring students succeed on it. The discrimination for such an item would be +1.00

An item discriminates negatively if more lowest-scoring than highest-scoring students respond correctly. Such items often have serious problems and need to be revised or discarded. Maximum negative discrimination occurs when all lowest-scoring students respond correctly to the item and no highest-scoring students succeed on it. The discrimination for such an item would be -1.00. This is a rare situation.

A discrimination of 0.00 (no discrimination) would be reported for an item to which an equal number of highest- and lowest-scoring students respond correctly. Such an item should be reviewed and in all likelihood rewritten because it does not differentiate between the two groups.

EXAMPLE 4.6

Number of students from the highest- and lowest-scoring groups that responded correctly to each test item

Item	Highest 25%	Lowest 25%
1.	5	1
2.	2	4
3.	3	3

For a class size of 24 (in Example 4.6) six students (K = 25 percent of 24 or K = 6) were identified in the highest- and lowest-scoring groups. Item 1 shows that five students from the highest-scoring group (H=5) and one student from the lowest-scoring group (L=1) responded correctly. This item discriminates positively, since more students from the highest than from the lowest group responded correctly.

$$\text{Item discrimination} = \frac{H - L}{K}$$

$$\text{Item discrimination} = \frac{5 - 1}{6} = .67$$

Item 2 discriminates negatively, since more students from the lowest than from the highest group responded correctly.

$$\text{Item discrimination} = \frac{2 - 4}{6} = -.33$$

Item 3 shows no discrimination, since an equal number of students from both groups responded correctly.

$$\text{Item discrimination} = \frac{3 - 3}{6} = .00$$

If computer analysis is available, a more detailed item response profile using the responses from both groups can be prepared to analyze the attractiveness (effectiveness) of each multiple-choice alternative. Normally, a good distractor attracts more lowest- than highest-scoring students.

EXAMPLE 4.7

Test Item

The design principle that stresses the use of contrasting elements so controlled and placed as to hold and retain attention is

    *1. balance.
    2. variety.
    3. unity.
    4. proportion.

Response Profile

*1	2	3	4	(Alternatives)
5	4	0	1	(# of H responses)
1	2	0	7	(# of L responses)

Item Discrimination

$$\text{Item discrimination} = \frac{5-1}{10} = \frac{4}{10} = .40$$

For a class size of 40 (in Example 4.7), ten students (K = 25 percent of 40 or K = 10) were identified in the highest- and lowest-scoring groups. The response profile reveals that the correct choice is alternative 1, and the item discrimination is positive, since five highest-scoring students and one lowest-scoring student responded correctly. Further examination shows alternative 2 to be a poor distractor, since it attracted more highest- than lowest-scoring students. Alternative 3 is ineffective, since it attracted no students from either group. Alternative 4 is an effective distractor because it attracted more lowest- than highest-scoring students. This information assists teachers in determining which distractors (if any) are adequately attracting more lowest- than highest-scoring students. By analyzing test items in this manner, teachers can improve the entire test.

Example 4.8 is based on a class of 40 students (10 in the highest and lowest groups); it illustrates item difficulty and discrimination.

EXAMPLE 4.8

Item Difficulty and Discrimination

Item No.	Item Difficulty	Item Discrimination
1	.60	.50
2	.40	.00
3	.20	.30
4	.10	−.10
5	.90	.10

Difficulty for the items in the preceding example can be interpreted as follows:

- Items 1 and 2: Moderate difficulty (.30 to .70)
- Items 3 and 4: High difficulty (.30 or less)
- Item 5: Low difficulty (.70 or greater).

Discrimination for these items can be interpreted as follows:

- Item 1: High discrimination (.40 or higher)
- Item 3: Moderate discrimination (.30 to .40)
- Items 2 and 5: Very low discrimination (.20 or less)
- Item 4: Negative discrimination (examine for revision).

Such information about item difficulty and discrimination on existing tests will assist teachers in writing better test items that will ultimately result in a more accurate assessment of student achievement.

Chapter 5

Desirable Characteristics of Tests

All classroom teachers should be concerned that tests provide results that are valid and reliable measures of student performance. An understanding of the procedures used to determine validity and reliability is necessary to assess the test as a whole.

VALIDITY

Validity refers to the extent to which a test measures what it was intended to measure; it is the most important requisite of any test. Even though other practical and technical considerations are satisfactory, the test has doubtful value without supportive evidence of validity.

The four major types of validity commonly used with teacher-made tests are content, construct, concurrent, and predictive. Each type requires a specific procedure and has a primary use.

EXAMPLE 5.1

Types of Test Validity

Type	Procedure	Primary Use
Content	Compares test items with instructional objectives	Assessment of test content
Construct	Identifies underlying concepts measured by test	Assessment of test adequacy
Concurrent	Compares test with another similar measure of present performance	Provision of substitute test for less convenient existing measure
Predictive	Compares test performance with future outcome	Selection and classification of students

---

Content Validity

Content validity, the most common type of validation used by teachers, ascertains that the test provides an accurate assessment of the instructional objectives. No empirical procedures are used to establish content validity. Rather, test items are individually analyzed and compared with the levels of behavior specified in the instructional objectives.

A useful aid for teachers attempting to establish content validity is a reading level word list—a published list that indicates an average student's reading level for a specific age or grade. Such a checking device can ensure that the vocabulary used in the test item is not an obstacle to students.

Construct Validity

Construct validity identifies the psychological traits or underlying constructs of a test. Constructs are hypothetical qualities that are assumed to exist in order to account for behavior in varying situations. In essence, this type of validity asks the question, "What is the test actually measuring?" For example, in a test developed to measure a mentally retarded student's ability to use metric linear concepts (Example 5.2), the constructs might consist of (1) assigning and recognizing metric symbols, (2) assigning and recognizing metric values, (3) associative conceptualization of scale numbers to measurement lengths, (4) psychomotor ability to measure objects with a metric scale and conceptualize with length measurements, and (5) test-taking ability that would include the following:

- Attention span
- Familiarity with mechanics of test (following directions, etc.)
- Test-wise ability (experience in test taking)
- Transferability of answers to response sheet.

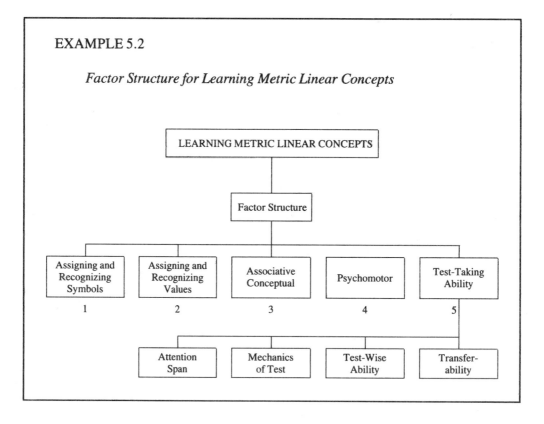

EXAMPLE 5.2

Factor Structure for Learning Metric Linear Concepts

Concurrent Validity

Concurrent validity compares a teacher-made test with another assessment measure. A major reason for establishing concurrent validity is to substitute a test for a more time-consuming or more complex instrument.

Predictive Validity

Predictive validity correlates test performance with some future outcome—for example, using ninth grade Scholastic Aptitude Test scores to predict success in tenth grade high school chemistry. Both concurrent and predictive validity rely on correlation coefficients or an expectancy table to indicate the degree of relationship.

Suppose a teacher is interested in determining the usefulness of a mathematics aptitude test (administered at the beginning of the school year) to predict final test grades in Algebra I. To determine if the two measures are related, the teacher prepares an expectancy table.

EXAMPLE 5.3

Expectancy Table

Mathematics Aptitude Test Scores and
Final Test Grades in Algebra I

| \[Mathematics Aptitude Test Scores \] | | | | | Test |
2–5	6–9	10–13	14–17	18–21	Grades
		1	3	3	7 A's
		10	1	4	15 B's
	4	6	2	1	13 C's
	4	1			5 D's
1	3				4 F's
1	11	18	6	8	44

$r = .66$

An examination of the expectancy table in example 5.3 reveals that the grades on the final test are 7 A's, 15 B's, 13 C's, 5 D's, and 4 F's. Eight of the 44 students had the highest mathematics aptitude test scores (between 18 and 21); six students had aptitude test scores between 14 and 17. Of these 14 students receiving the highest scores, 11 (79 percent) received final test grades of A or B. All 14 students received final test grades of C or higher.

Further examination of the table indicates that 7 of the 11 students (64 percent) with aptitude test scores between 6 and 9 had final grades of D or F. In addition, 31 of 32 students (97 percent) with aptitude scores of 10 or greater had final test grades of A, B, or C.

The correlation coefficient calculated for these two measures is .66. The analysis of the table indicates modest predictive validity for the test scores.

RELIABILITY

Next to validity, reliability is the most important characteristic of a test. Without reliability, little confidence can be placed in test results. A test that is not valid, but highly reliable, may measure something irrelevant with great precision. Reliability provides an estimate of the consistency of the test results; it is expressed as a correlation coefficient reported on a scale ranging from 0.00 to 1.00. Teachers should not, however, expect test results to be perfectly consistent. As a test is administered to different students and/or groups, variations in test scores can be expected because of factors other than quality (for example, fatigue, guessing). Generally, however, if reliability is high, a second administration of a similar test to the same students should produce similar scores. If reliability is low, it is doubtful that two administrations of the same test would produce similar scores.

Reliability coefficients used with teacher-made tests are usually identified by the method used to calculate the reliability. These methods are test-retest, equivalent forms, split-half, and Kuder-Richardson. Each method follows specific procedures and provides evidence of a type of consistency.

EXAMPLE 5.4

Types of Test Reliability

Method	Procedure	Type of Consistency
Test-Retest	Correlates scores for two administrations of same test. Second administration at later time, i.e., one month, one-half year.	Stability of test results over time
Equivalent Forms	Correlates scores for two forms of test.	Equivalency of forms
Split-Half	Correlates scores for two halves of test. Applies correction formula.	Internal test consistency
Kuder-Richardson Formula 21	Calculates mean and standard deviation of test scores. Computes reliability coefficient.	Internal test consistency

---

Test-Retest

The test-retest method requires two administrations of the same test to the same group of students in a given time interval. The interval may vary from a few days to several years, depending on the use of the results. If the results show that students' scores were approximately the same on both administrations of the test, then a positive relationship would exist (1.00 indicates a perfect positive relationship and 0.00 indicates no relationship). The test-retest method is seldom used to establish reliability for teacher-made tests because of the requirement of administering the test twice to the same students.

Equivalent Forms

The equivalent forms method of establishing reliability requires the administration of two different, but equivalent, forms of a test. The two tests are administered to the same students and the scores are correlated. The correlation provides an estimate of how well both forms of the test assess the same instructional objectives.

Split-Half

The split-half method of establishing reliabilty requires the use of two halves of the same test. The usual practice involves correlating scores from the odd- and even-numbered test items. The correlation coefficient provides a measure of internal consistency and indicates the equivalency of the two halves in assessing the instructional objectives. Finally, a correction formula (Spearman-Brown) is applied to the correlation coefficient, which establishes a reliability coefficient for the entire test.

FORMULA

Spearman-Brown Formula

$$\text{Reliability of entire test} = \frac{2 \times \text{Reliability on 1/2 test}}{1 + \text{Reliability on 1/2 test}}$$

If, for example, the half-tests correlated .50, then the correlation coefficient of the whole test would be .67.

EXAMPLE 5.5

$$\text{Reliability of entire test} = \frac{2 \times .50}{1 + .50} = \frac{1.00}{1.50} = .67$$

Kuder-Richardson

The Kuder-Richardson (Formula 21) method of calculating reliability requires a single administration of the test and uses the mean and standard deviation of the test scores.

FORMULA

Kuder-Richardson Formula 21 (KR21)

$$KR21 = \frac{A}{A-1}\left(1 - \frac{X(A - \overline{X})}{A(SD)^2}\right)$$

A = test length (# of items)

$\overline{X}$ = mean of the test scores

SD = standard deviation of the test scores

If, for example, a distribution of test scores for a 50-item test has a mean of 30 and a standard deviation of 6, the KR21 reliability is .68.

EXAMPLE 5.6

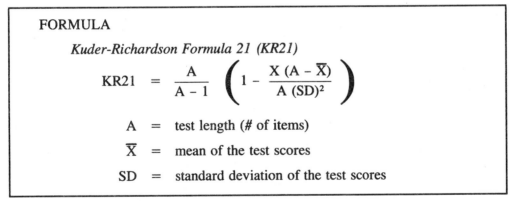

$$KR21 = \frac{50}{49}\left(1 - \frac{30(50 - 30)}{50(6)^2}\right) = .68$$

The KR21 is easily determined if the mean and standard deviation of the test scores have previously been calculated. This can be accomplished by a hand-held calculator or one of several statistic software programs used with microcomputers.

Improving Test Reliability

Several test characteristics affect reliability. They include the following:

- *Test length.* In general, a longer test will be more reliable than a shorter one because longer tests sample the instructional objectives more adequately. Considering this single factor, teachers should strive for longer tests whenever circumstances permit.

- *Spread of scores.* The type of students taking the test can influence reliability. A group of students with heterogeneous ability will produce a larger spread of test scores than will a group with homogeneous ability.

- *Item difficulty.* In general, tests composed of items of moderate difficulty (.30 to .70) will have more influence on reliability than those composed mainly of items that are easy or difficult.

- *Item discrimination.* In general, tests composed of more discriminating items will have greater reliability than those composed of less discriminating items.

- *Time limits.* Adding a time factor may improve reliability for lower-level cognitive test items. Since all students do not function at the same pace, a time factor adds another criterion to the test that causes discrimination, thus improving reliability. Teachers should not, however, arbitrarily impose a time limit on a test. For higher-level cognitive test items, the imposition of a time limit may defeat the intended purpose of the items.

Sample Verbs Used to Identify Specific Student Behaviors*

General Discriminative Behaviors

Choose	Describe	Discriminate	Indicate	Match	Place
Collect	Detect	Distinguish	Isolate	Omit	Point
Define	Differentiate	Identify	List	Order	Select

Study Behaviors

Arrange	Classify	Follow	Look	Organize	Sort
Categorize	Compile	Formulate	Map	Quote	Underline
Chart	Copy	Gather	Mark	Record	
Cite	Diagram	Itemize	Name	Reproduce	
Circle	Document	Label	Note	Search	

Analysis Behaviors

Analyze	Compare	Criticize	Evaluate	Generate	Plan
Appraise	Conclude	Deduce	Explain	Induce	Structure
Combine	Contrast	Defend	Formulate	Infer	

Creative Behaviors

Alter	Generalize	Rearrange	Rename	Restructue	Simplify
Ask	Paraphrase	Recombine	Reorder	Retell	Synthesize
Change	Predict	Reconstruct	Rephrase	Rewrite	Systematize
Design	Question	Regroup	Restate		

Miscellaneous Behaviors

Attempt	Discover	Grind	Position	Send	Suggest
Attend	Distribute	Hold	Present	Serve	Supply
Begin	End	Include	Produce	Sew	Support
Bring	Erase	Inform	Propose	Share	Switch
Buy	Expand	Lead	Provide	Sharpen	Take
Complete	Extend	Lend	Put	Shorten	Tear
Consider	Find	Light	Raise	Shut	Touch
Correct	Finish	Make	Relate	Signify	Type
Crush	Fit	Mend	Repeat	Start	Use
Designate	Fix	Miss	Return	Store	Vote
Develop	Get	Offer	Save	Strike	

---

*From C. K. Claus, ''Verbs and Imperative Sentences as a Basis for Stating Educational Objectives.'' Paper given at meeting of National Council on Measurement in Education, Chicago, 1968.

Appendix B

Sample Verbs Used in Various Curriculum Areas*

Art Behaviors

Assemble	Construct	Illustrate	Mold	Pour	Sculpt
Carve	Draw	Melt	Paint	Press	Sketch
Color	Fold	Mix	Paste	Roll	Trace

Drama Behaviors

Cross	Display	Exit	Move	Pass	Sit
Direct	Enter	Leave	Pantomime	Proceed	Turn

Language Behaviors

Accent	Hyphenate	Pronounce	Speak	Summarize	Verbalize
Alphabetize	Indent	Punctuate	Spell	Syllabicate	Whisper
Edit	Outline	Read	State	Translate	Write

Laboratory Science Behaviors

Calibrate	Convert	Dissect	Increase	Manipulate	Report
Conduct	Decrease	Feed	Lengthen	Prepare	Specify
Connect	Demonstrate	Grow	Limit	Remove	Weigh

Mathematical Behaviors

Add	Divide	Graph	Interpolate	Prove	Square
Bisect	Estimate	Group	Measure	Reduce	Tabulate
Calculate	Extrapolate	Integrate	Multiply	Solve	Verify

Music Behaviors

Blow	Compose	Hum	Pluck	Sing	Tap
Bow	Finger	Mute	Practice	Strum	Whistle
Clap	Harmonize	Play			

Physical Behaviors

Bend	Hit	Kick	Run	Somersault	Swing
Catch	Hop	March	Skate	Stretch	Throw
Grasp	Jump	Pitch	Skip	Swim	Walk

Social Behaviors

Agree	Compliment	Disagree	Greet	Join	Participate
Answer	Contribute	Discuss	Help	Laugh	Praise
Argue	Cooperate	Forgive	Invite	Meet	Smile

*From C. K. Claus, ''Verbs and Imperative Sentences as a Basis for Stating Educational Objectives.'' Paper given at meeting of National Council on Measurement in Education, Chicago, 1968.

Sample Test Items

This appendix presents sample test items from the following curriculum areas: Art, Biology, Chemistry, English, Foreign Language, Home Economics, Industrial Arts, Mathematics, Music, Physical Education, Physics, Science, and Social Studies. Most of these areas include the four types of test items discussed in this text (true-false, multiple-choice, matching, and essay); others include selected types of test items. This does not mean that any type of test item cannot be used in all the areas mentioned; on the contrary, the authors of the sample items made the decision to use the material that appears here for their curriculum areas.

Several of the sample test items that follow were contributed by secondary teachers from the Price Laboratory School on the campus of the University of Northern Iowa; some of these were prepared in collaboration with faculty members of the university. They were collected and organized by David Lickteig, Assistant Professor, University of Northern Iowa. The remaining items were obtained from the files of other secondary teachers; they were arranged by the authors to provide a consistent format.

Sample Test Items
for
ART

True-False Items

_T_ 1. Picasso was a Spanish painter known for his cubist paintings.

_T_ 2. Value studies in painting involve mixing white or black with a particular color to produce tints and shades of that color.

_T_ 3. VanGogh was a Dutch painter known for his short, choppy brush strokes.

_F_ 4. Jan and Hubert Vermeer were the Flemish painters who introduced oil painting in Europe in the early 1400s.

_F_ 5. Linear drawing is concerned strictly with the hand working with the eye.

Multiple-Choice Items

1. The artist known for painting "The Last Supper" and the "Mona Lisa" is
    1. Rembrandt.
    2. Michelangelo.
    *3. da Vinci.
    4. Raphael.

2. The Spanish artist known for his elongation of figures and combining and contrasting of light and dark areas to look like reflections and shadows from a special lighting effect is
    *1. El Greco.
    2. Gauguin.
    3. Giotto.
    4. Velazquez.

3. A woodcut is an example of which of the following processes?
    1. aquatint
    2. embossing
    3. intaglio
    *4. relief

4. The American artist known for painting "American Gothic" is
    1. Marin.
    *2. Wood.
    3. Ryder.
    4. Sargent.

Matching Items

I	II
__4__ 1. Style is depicted by means of exaggerations and distortions in line and color, the abandonment of naturalism.	1. Abstractionism
	2. Cubism
__2__ 2. A style of art that involves both the manipulation of the mind and the manipulation of materials. It is characterized by arbitrary planes, textures, and colors, often depicting subjects from several different viewpoints at once.	3. Dadaism
	4. Expressionism
	5. Impressionism
__6__ 3. Optical mixture of colors developed by Seurat.	6. Pointillism
__5__ 4. An artistic movement depicting subjects in natural settings, its main concern being the effect of light upon color.	

Essay Item

Discuss six ways that artists show distance in their work.

Points for grading

- Converging lines (1 point)
- Overlapping (1 point)
- Less detail in distant subjects and more in closer ones (1 point)
- Graying the colors of subjects in the distance (1 point)
- Making close subjects larger and far subjects smaller (1 point)
- Placing more distant subjects higher in the picture, e.g., oriental painters (1 point)

Sample items were prepared by Ardith Hoff, Cedar Falls Public Schools, Cedar Falls, Iowa.

Sample Test Items
for
BIOLOGY

True-False Items

F   1. Plants are capable of losing water by a process called *dehydration* through the vascular bundles.

T   2. Diseases are defined as a change from the normal state preventing specific organs from carrying out their specific functions.

F   3. A substance that releases hydroxyl ions when dissolved in water or that can give off protons when reacting chemically is called a base.

T   4. During the dark stage of photosynthesis, the energy produced during the light phase is converted into sugar and oxygen through chemical reactions that do not involve light.

T   5. A catalyst is a substance that stimulates a chemical reaction to occur by lowering the activation energy requirement and that does not become a part of the final product.

Multiple-Choice Items

1. A basic determiner of heredity is
    1. amino acid.
    *2. DNA.
    3. mutation.
    4. RNA.

2. An example of an inherited gene mutation in humans is
    1. exposure to radiation.
    2. replication of DNA.
    *3. sickle cell anemia.
    4. synthesis of proteins.

3. A peptide bond forms between
    *1. the carboxyl group of one amino acid and the amino group of another amino acid.
    2. the carboxyl groups of two amino acids.
    3. two amino acids with the addition of a water molecule.
    4. an amino acid and a carbohydrate with the loss of a water molecule.

4. The probability of a family having a girl and two boys in that order is
    1. 1/3.
    2. 1/2.
    3. 1/6.
    *4. 1/8.

The following diagram represents a trait for albinism. Individuals who are albinos are represented by filled-in circles.

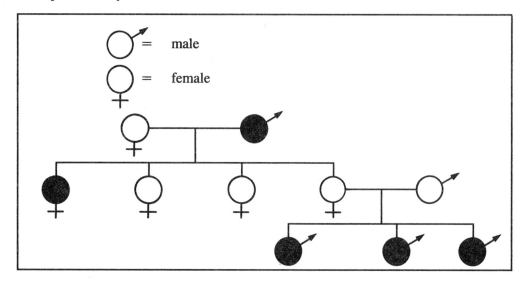

5. From studying the preceding diagram, one can determine that
    *1. albinism is a recessive trait.
    2. albinism is a dominant trait.
    3. albinism affects only men.
    4. albinism is passed on by only one parent.

Matching Items

I	II
__5__ 1. Hemophilia	1. Autosome dominant
__2__ 2. Sickle-cell anemia and cystic fibrosis	2. Autosome recessive
__4__ 3. Down's syndrome	3. Polyfactorial
	4. Trisomy
	5. X-linked recessive gene

Essay Item

Each year thousands of salmon return to the same freshwater spawning area where they had their beginning. How they know where to go is still a mystery. However, the migration toward freshwater seems to have a more concrete concept behind it. One suggestion is that hormones found in the cells of the salmon affect the existing osmotic conditions between the cells and the surrounding sea water. It is possible that the hormones secreted in the cells of the fish are synchronized with spawning. Discuss spawning migration in terms of existing osmotic conditions and the secretion of specific hormones.

Points for grading

● Relating answer to general comments about osmosis (2 points)
● Relating osmosis to the conditions between salmon and sea water (3 points)

Sample test items were prepared by James Kelly, Price Laboratory School, University of Northern Iowa, Cedar Falls.

Sample Test Items
for
CHEMISTRY

True-False Items

__T__   1. The chemical behaviors of sodium and cesium are quite similar.

__F__   2. Since an atom is electrically neutral, the number of protons is equal to the number of neutrons.

__F__   3. The chloride ion consists of 17 protons, 18 neutrons, and 18 electrons.

__T__   4. The algebraic sum of the oxidation numbers of the atoms in the formula of a compound is zero.

__T__   5. A covalent bond is formed in the diatomic hydrogen molecule.

Multiple-Choice Items

1. A vertical column of elements in the periodic table is known as a/an
   - *1. family.
   - 2. ocet.
   - 3. period.
   - 4. series

2. The element capable of replacing all others in the halogen family is
   - 1. bromine.
   - 2. chlorine.
   - *3. fluorine.
   - 4. iodine.

3. The oxidation number of phosphorous in the polyatomic ion PO_43+ is
   - 1. 3+
   - *2. 5+
   - 3. 2+
   - 4. 4+

4. The number of moles of aluminum atoms reacting with three moles of oxyge‑ molecules in the equation $4A1 + 3O_2 ⭡ 2A1_2O_3$ is
   - 1. 1
   - 2. 2
   - 3. 3
   - *4. 4

5. The number of moles in one kilogram of zinc is
   - 1. 14.1
   - *2. 15.1
   - 3. 16.5
   - 4. 33.3

Matching Items

	I		II
7	1. A substance that does the dissolving.		1. distillation
2	2. Two liquids that do not dissolve in each other.		2. immiscible
4	3. Substance of low solubility.		3. miscible
1	4. A method of purifying a substance.		4. precipitate
6	5. The substance being dissolved.		5. soluble
			6. solute
			7. solvent

Essay Item

In the equation $2NaClO_3 \rightarrow 2NaCl + 3O_2$, how many grams of $NaClO_3$ are required to produce one mole of O_2?

Points for grading

- Answer: 70.7g (3 points)

Sample test items were prepared by Norman E. Anderson, Cedar Falls High School, Cedar Falls, Iowa.

Sample Test Items
for
ENGLISH

True-False Items

__F__   1. A METICULOUS dresser would wear a tie with a food stain.

__F__   2. A COMPASSIONATE person would let a stray dog go hungry.

__T__   3. When Joe spoke SCOFFINGLY of Karen, he was ridiculing her.

__T__   4. Your school is COEDUCATIONAL.

__F__   5. You would be likely to carry a RUCKSACK to the prom.

Multiple-Choice Items

Act II, Scenes 1 and 2: *Diary of Anne Frank*

1. The Franks had been in hiding
    1. three months.
    2. six months.
    *3. eighteen months.
    4. three years.

2. What did Miep bring to celebrate the New Year?
    *1. cake
    2. cookies
    3. ice cream
    4. pie

3. Rations were cut because
    1. food was being hoarded.
    2. food was scarce.
    3. more Jews had joined those already in the Annex.
    *4. the suppliers of ration books were arrested.

4. Mr. VanDaan decided to sell
    1. Peter's cat.
    *2. his wife's coat.
    3. his supply of cigarettes.
    4. his ring.

5. What happened to Mr. Kraler?
    1. He was questioned by the police.
    2. He was deported.
    *3. He was hospitalized.
    4. He was killed.

Matching Items

	I		II
5	1. irrational fear		1. acrimony
3	2. lack of seriousness		2. canton
4	3. edible fish		3. levity
2	4. small district		4. mullet
1	5. harsh manner		5. phobia

Essay Items

1. Laertes and Hamlet are often regarded as opposites. Write a paragraph illustrating their differences. Include at least three contrasting characteristics.

    Points for grading

    - Contrasting characteristics (3 points)
    - Illustrating differences (4 points)
    - Quality and organization (3 points)

2. Hamlet's personality makeup is at one time intense, complex, contemplative, and dynamic. How would you defend such a statement?

    Points for grading

    - Defense of statement (6 points)
    - Quality and organization (2 points)

Sample test items were prepared by Jane Wilson, former English teacher, Price Laboratory School, University of Northern Iowa, Cedar Falls.

Sample Test Items
for
FOREIGN LANGUAGE

True-False Items

__T__   1. Voici un livre.
       (Here is a book.)

__F__   2. Voici une maison.
       (Here is a house.)

Read the following French passage and answer the questions.

Les parents de Pierre ne se sont pas levés aujourd'hui parce qu'ils se sont couchés très tard hier soir après leur surprise-party. Quelle chance pour eux parce que c'est samedi et M. Dubois n'a pas besoin d'aller au bureau.

(Pierre's parents did not get up early today because they went to bed very late last night after their party. What luck for them because it is Saturday and Mr. Dubois does not need to go to the office.)

__T__   3. Les parents de Pierre sont encore couchés au lit. (Pierre's parents are still in bed.)

__F__   4. Ils doivent travailler aujourd'hui. (They have to work today.)

__F__   5. C'est samedi et il y a une surprise-party ce soir. (It is Saturday and there is a party tonight.)

Multiple-Choice Items

Read the following French passage and answer the questions.

Madame Dupont est à la maison. Ce soir elle a décidé de préparer de la soupe à l'oignon pour le dîner. Ce matin elle a acheté des oignons au marché et maintenant elle va préparer cette soupe délicieuse pour sa famille. Toute sa famille aime la soupe à l'oignon sauf son fils Jean-Luc. Sans doute il va manger des frites et un hot dog au lieu de cette soupe.

(Mrs. Dupont is at home. She has decided to make onion soup for dinner this evening. She bought some onions at the market this morning and is now going to prepare this delicious soup for her family. The whole family likes onion soup except her son Jean-Luc. No doubt he will eat French fries and a hot dog instead of the soup.)

---

1. Où est Madame Dupont? (Where is Mrs. Dupont?)
    1. Elle est au marché. (She is at the market.)
    2. Elle est à table. (She is at the table.)
    *3. Elle est chez elle. (She is at home.)
    4. Elle est dans la cuisine. (She is in the kitchen.)

2. Qu est-ce qu'elle va préparer ce soir? (What is she going to prepare tonight?)
    *1. De la soupe à l'oignon. (Onion soup)
    2. Des frites. (French fries)
    3. Des hots dogs. (Hot dogs)
    4. Un hot dog délicieux. (A delicious hot dog)

3. Est-ce que toute la famille aime cette soupe? (Does everyone like this soup?)
    1. Oui, tout le monde l'aime. (Yes, everyone likes it.)
    2. Oui, mais pas son mari. (Yes, but not her husband.)
    *3. Non, pas son fils. (No, not her son.)
    4. Non, sa fille ne l'aime pas beaucoup. (No, her daughter does not like it much.)

Essay Items

1. Describe in Spanish a typical family meal at your house.

    Points for grading

    ● Proper spelling and use of food and drink items (5 points)
    ● Good composition (5 points)

2. Describe in Spanish an incident in your life when you were young. Be sure to pay special attention to the use of the imperfect and the past definite tenses. Include how the incident happened, where, why, and the consequences. This paper should be at least one page in length.

    Points for grading

    ● The incident identifies the how, where, why, and the consequences (10 points).
    ● The incident includes proper imperfect and past definite tenses (10 points).
    ● The paper is at least one page in length (5 points).

Sample test items were prepared by James E. Becker, Modern Language Department, University of Northern Iowa, Cedar Falls.

Sample Test Items
for
HOME ECONOMICS

True-False Items

___T___ 1. Cottage cheese, yogurt, and ice cream are examples of choices from the milk group of the basic four food groups.

___F___ 2. Peanut butter, whole wheat bread, and ground beef are included in the meat group.

___T___ 3. One medium whole fruit or one-half cup of cooked vegetables equals one serving from the fruit/vegetable group.

___T___ 4. Citrus fruits include oranges, grapefruit, and tangerines.

___T___ 5. Four or more daily servings are needed of foods from the bread and cereal group.

Multiple-Choice Items

1. Which of the following is not a synthetic fiber?
   - 1. acetate
   - *2. linen
   - 3. nylon
   - 4. polyester

2. Fabrics that use the twill weave are
   - *1. denim and gabardine.
   - 2. gabardine and nylon.
   - 3. gingham and nylon.
   - 4. nylon and linen.

3. Which of the following is not a type of sleeve?
   - 1. cap
   - *2. middy
   - 3. raglan
   - 4. set-in

4. Lines used in clothing design to create a feeling of height and slimness are
   - 1. diagonal.
   - 2. horizontal.
   - *3. vertical.
   - 4. curvy.

5. A natural fiber is

      1. acrylic.
      2. rayon.
      3. triacetate.
   *4. wool.

Matching Items

	I		II
7	1. processing method for low acid foods		1. blanching
2	2. processing method for high acid foods		2. boiling water bath
5	3. meats and vegetables		3. high acid foods
6	4. canning method recommended only for jellies		4. hot pack
3	5. fruits, pickles, tomatoes		5. low acid foods
			6. open kettle method
			7. pressure canner
			8. raw or cold pack

Essay Item

Knowing how to make white sauce is a very important food preparation skill. Explain the correct procedure for preparing a basic white sauce, including ingredients, and three or more ways to use it.

Points for grading

- The procedure is clear and understandable (8 points).
- The ingredients are correctly stated (6 points).
- Three or more uses are noted (6 points).

Sample test items were prepared by Judy Tucker, Bettsville Local Schools, Bettsville, Ohio.

Sample Test Items
for
INDUSTRIAL ARTS

True-False Items

__T__   1. A number 4 wood screw is smaller in diameter than a number 10 wood screw.

__F__   2. An abrasive paper grit size 120 is coarser than an abrasive paper grit size 80.

__F__   3. Plywood, particle board, and hardboard are purchased by board feet.

__T__   4. An 8d nail is 2½'' long.

__F__   5. An auger bit stamped 12 on the tang would bore a hole 7/8''.

Multiple-Choice Items

1. A process of hammering and squeezing metal (usually heated) into a required shape is
    1. casting.
    2. extruding.
    *3. forging.
    4. machining.

2. A metal casting process that produces a very fine finish is
    1. centrifugal.
    2. full mold.
    3. green sand.
    *4. investment.

3. The slot that is made in wood when sawing is called the
    1. groove.
    *2. kerf.
    3. kreft.
    4. rake.

4. The two methods of drying lumber are air drying and
    1. age drying.
    2. chemical drying.
    3. evaporation drying.
    *4. kiln drying.

5. The solvent for shellac is
    *1. alcohol.
    2. lacquer thinner.
    3. turpentine.
    4. water.

Matching Items

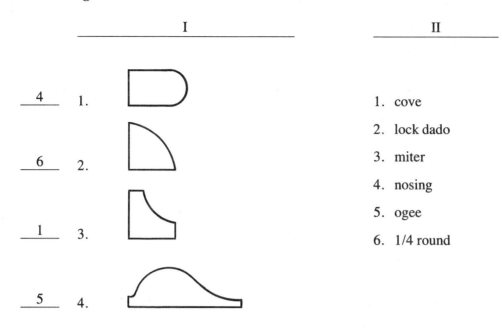

	I		II
__4__	1.		1. cove
__6__	2.		2. lock dado
__1__	3.		3. miter
__5__	4.		4. nosing
			5. ogee
			6. 1/4 round

Essay Item

Describe the difference between continuous and intermittent manufacturing.

Points for grading

- Key words (continuous and intermittent) are defined (10 points).
- Each manufacturing type is clearly distinguished from the other (20 points).

Sample test items were prepared by Leslie C. Miller III, Department of Industrial Technology, University of Northern Iowa, and Duane H. Rippe, Holmes Junior High School, Cedar Falls.

Sample Test Items
for
MATHEMATICS

True-False Items

__F__   1. If x is a positive number, then $\sqrt{x}$ is less than x.

__T__   2. The expression $3x - 2 - 2(3x - 7)$ is equal to $-3x + 12$.

__T__   3. The product $(3a + 5)(a - 1)$ equals $3a^2 + 2a - 5$.

__F__   4. If triangle ABC is isosceles and A is 100°, then B is 100°.

__F__   5. Seven is a factor of 17.

Multiple-Choice Items

1. The diameter of one circle is 6 cm and the diameter of another circle is 12 c⸍
   How many cm larger is the area of one circle than the other?

       1. 3π cm²
       2. 6π cm²
   *3. 27π cm²
       4. 108π cm²

2. A heptagon has how many sides?

       1. 5
       2. 6
   *3. 7
       4. 8

3. What is the expanded product of $(2x - 4)$ and $(x + 1)$?

       1. $2x^2 - 4$
       2. $2x^2 + 4$
       3. $2x^2 + 2x + 4$
   *4. $2x^2 - 2x - 4$

4. If $9 - a = 0.5a$, what does a equal?

       1. 0.4
   *2. 6.0
       3. 8.5
       4. 9.5

5. If $2x - 5 = 7x - 15$, what does x equal?

       1. 4
   *2. 2
       3. 0
       4. -2

6. In a basketball game, Jessica made 75% of her 12 free throw attempts. Leanne made 60% of her 10 free throw attempts. How many more free throws did Jessica make than Leanne?

    1. 1
    2. 2
    *3. 3
    4. 4

7. A park in the shape of a rectangle is 325 meters long and 100 meters wide. What is the measure of the perimeter of the park?

    *1. 850 meters
    2. 750 meters
    3. 525 meters
    4. 425 meters

Matching Items

	I		II
6	1. 3/4		1. 0.060
3	2. 3/5		2. 0.500
4	3. 5/8		3. 0.600
1	4. 3/50		4. 0.625
2	5. 13/26		5. 0.670
			6. 0.750
			7. 0.875

Sample test items were prepared by John Tarr, Price Laboratory School, University of Northern Iowa, Cedar Falls.

Sample Test Items
for
MUSIC

True-False Items

F	1.	The most likely meter for the example above would be 2/4.
T	2.	A performer will adjust the dynamic written markings to fit various performance conditions.
F	3.	Accurate tuning of one's instrument to concert B flat assures that other notes will be played in tune.
F	4.	A key signature containing three flats indicates that the music to follow is in the key of E flat.

Multiple-Choice Items

1. Which music direction is *least* likely to appear in the famous march "The Thunderer" (Sousa)?

    1. tacet 1X
    2. simile
    3. marcato
  *4. con sordino

2. Which of the following sets shows tempo markings in a correct slow to fast order?

    1. andante-adagio-vivace
    2. allegro-andante-presto
  *3. largo-moderato-allegro
    4. andante-largo-presto

3. The preceding example appears to be scored for which combination of instruments (in score order)?

    1. trumpet-horn-trombone
*2. violin-clarinet-cello
    3. flute-clarinet-string bass
    4. violin-viola-cello

Matching Items

You will hear five short excerpts (about 45 second each) of unfamiliar concert band pieces. Use the clues provided with each title to match the pieces with the example numbers.

	I	II
_____	1. *Ecossaise* (Beethoven): homophonic texture, strong accents, repetition of short sections, detached style.	1. 1st excerpt 2. 2d excerpt
_____	2. "Siciliana" from *A Little Concert Suite* (Reed): compound meter, legato style, melody predominantly set in woodwinds, homophonic texture.	3. 3d excerpt
_____	3. *Lyric Essay* (Coakley): legato style, polyphonic texture, duple meter, brief baritone solo.	4. 4th excerpt
_____	4. "A Toye" from *Giles Farnaby Suite* (arr. Wiggins): alternating homophonic and polyphonic textures, duple meter, minor mode, mixture of detached and legato.	5. 5th excerpt
_____	5. *Scottish Rhapsody* (Grundman): colorful effects, use of folksong material, meter changes, unusual voicings.	

Essay Item

Most successful pieces of music show a balance between contrast and repetition. Why?

Points for grading

Structure (20 points maximum)

- The perception of organization in music, an aural event taking place across time, seems necessary for the enjoyment of music (5 points).

- Repetition and contrast are essential elements of musical organization and structure (5 points).

- Repetition and contrast may help define organization and structure at several levels (5 points).

- The elements of music used to create repetition and contrast may include rhythm, melody, harmony, timbre, and form (1 point for each element).

Mixture of novel and known (15 points maximum)

- Humans seem to find stimuli that are a mixture of novel and known information to be the most interesting (5 points).

- Too much novel information in a musical work is often perceived as chaotic (5 points); too much repetition is perceived as boring, dry, or academic (5 points).

Sample test items were prepared by Mark Ellis, Price Laboratory School, University of Northern Iowa, Cedar Falls.

Sample Test Items
for
PHYSICAL EDUCATION

True-False Items

__T__   1. In tennis, a score of zero is called love.

__F__   2. In tennis, a set consists of any combination of six total games.

__F__   3. If one player has won two points and the other player one point, the score is 40–30.

__T__   4. If a tennis player who has the advantage loses the next point, the score is deuce.

__T__   5. The point won after deuce is called advantage.

Multiple-Choice Items

1. When playing soccer, which method of trapping makes it easier to move the ball sideways?
    - *1. inside of the foot
    - 2. inside of the thigh
    - 3. shins
    - 4. sole of the foot

2. When a body part traps a soccer ball, it
    - *1. absorbs the full force of the ball.
    - 2. angles the ball down.
    - 3. angles the ball up.
    - 4. moves the ball to another player.

3. In a soccer game, what is the award if the ball touches an offensive player before going over the end line outside the goal?
    - 1. throw-in
    - 2. corner kick
    - *3. goal kick
    - 4. indirect free kick

4. The soccer player credited with doing the most running is the
    - 1. winger.
    - 2. right fullback.
    - 3. inside forward.
    - *4. center forward.

5. In field hockey, which player marks the right inner?
    - 1. right fullback
    - *2. left fullback
    - 3. right halfback
    - 4. center halfback

Matching Items

	I		II
_3_	1. Divides body into ventral and dorsal.		1. Bursa
_1_	2. Enables skin to slide freely over projecting bony surface.		2. Cartilage
_7_	3. Composed of dense collagenous tissue or almost pure elastic tissue.		3. Frontal plane
_6_	4. Part of the articular surface is rounded and the other shallowly concave.		4. Saddle
			5. Sagittal plane
_2_	5. Supporting tissue for softer tissue.		6. Spheroid joint
_4_	6. Type of joint found at base of thumb.		7. Tendon
			8. Tracts

Essay Item

Name the positions and describe the primary duties of each member of a regulation football team.

Points for grading

- All offensive team positions are named (10 points).
- Primary duties of each offensive teamplayer are adequately detailed (25 points).

Sample test items were prepared by Carol Phillips, Department of Health, Physical Education and Recreation, University of Northern Iowa; and John Aldrich, Price Laboratory School, University of Northern Iowa, Cedar Falls.

Sample Test Items
for
PHYSICS

True-False Items

__T__   1. 56 miles is a greater distance than 80 kilometers.

__T__   2. The slope of a velocity-time curve (graph) defines acceleration.

__F__   3. Constant speed and constant acceleration could be defined as the same motion.

__F__   4. Mass is a vector quantity.

__F__   5. Mass and weight are measured in the same units.

Multiple-Choice Items

1. In mechanics, three fundamental units are used to measure quantities. Which one of the following is *not* considered a fundamental unit?
    1. length
    2. mass
    *3. speed
    4. time

2. The number 0.003068 has how many significant digits?
    1. 3
    *2. 4
    3. 5
    4. 6

3. How do gravitational forces compare with electrical forces?
    *1. much smaller
    2. smaller
    3. much larger
    4. larger

4. In the impulse-momentum equation ft = mv, which variable is most important in the coach's request to ''follow through''?
    1. force (f)
    *2. time (t)
    3. mass (m)
    4. velocity (v)

5. Which of the following is a scalar quantity?
    1. acceleration
    2. force
    3. velocity
    *4. work

Matching Items

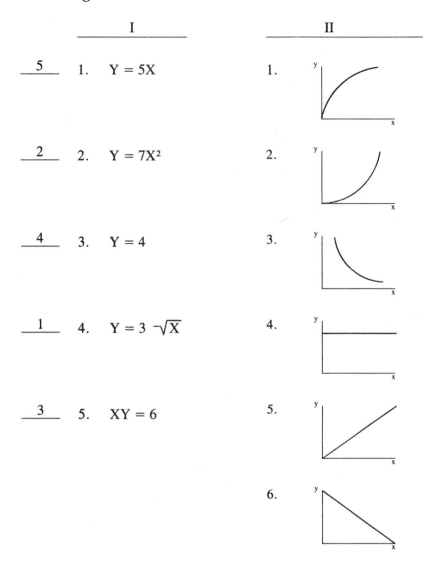

	I			II
_5_	1.	$Y = 5X$	1.	
_2_	2.	$Y = 7X^2$	2.	
_4_	3.	$Y = 4$	3.	
_1_	4.	$Y = 3\sqrt{X}$	4.	
_3_	5.	$XY = 6$	5.	
			6.	

Essay Item

A merry-go-round is 42 feet in diameter. It is making 5 complete revolutions in 2 minutes. A small child slips from a horse and falls off the edge. At what speed does the child hit the ground?

Points for Grading

- Correct Procedure (5 points).
- Answer: 5.5 ft./sec or 3.4 mph (5 points).

Sample test items were prepared by Oliver Eason, Cedar Falls High School, Iowa.

Sample Test Items
for
SCIENCE

True-False Items

__T__   1. The sun is the center of the solar system.

__F__   2. A light year measures time.

__F__   3. On a clear night, Polaris can be seen directly overhead.

__F__   4. The main fuel of a star is oxygen.

__T__   5. Jupiter is the largest planet in the solar system.

Multiple-Choice Items

1. The sun is a/an
- *1. middle-aged star.
- 2. old star.
- 3. young star.

2. A star's energy is produced by
- 1. burning.
- *2. fusion.
- 3. reflection.

3. The moon revolves around the earth in
- 1. 24 hours
- *2. 27⅓ days.
- 3. 365 days.

4. Meteoroids that reach the earth's surface are called
- 1. asteroids.
- *2. meteorites.
- 3. meteors.

5. Planets can be observed because they
- 1. burn.
- 2. give off their own light.
- *3. reflect the sun's light.

Matching Items

	I		II
_4_	1. A telescope that uses no light		1. reflecting parallax
_2_	2. Uses a concave mirror		2. reflecting telescope
_1_	3. A procedure for measuring star distance		3. refracting telescope
_3_	4. Uses a convex lens		4. radio telescope
_5_	5. Separates light into colors		5. spectroscope

Essay Item

How do astronomers know if galaxies are moving closer to or away from the earth?

Points for grading

- Doppler effect (1 point)
- Blue-shift in spectrum—toward (1 point)
- Red-shift in spectrum—away (1 point)

Sample test items were prepared by William Simpson, Peet Junior High School, Cedar Falls, Iowa.

Sample Test Items
for
SOCIAL STUDIES

True-False Items

__T__   1. Geographers have accepted the theory of ''Continental Drift'' as an explanation of past and present configurations of continents.

__T__   2. The climate of land next to large bodies of water will change less rapidly than the climate farther inland.

__F__   3. Humid tropical climates are found within five degrees latitude north and south of the Tropics of Cancer and Capricorn.

GRAPH BELOW RELATES TO STATEMENTS 4 and 5

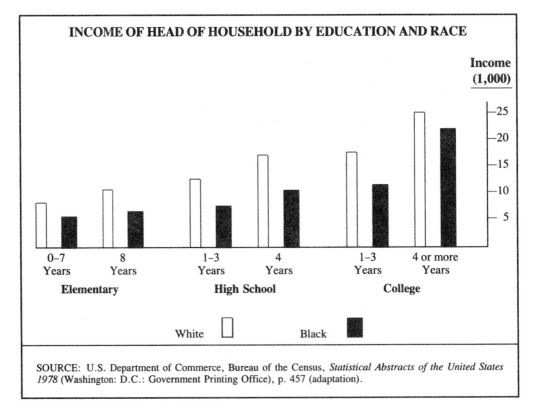

INCOME OF HEAD OF HOUSEHOLD BY EDUCATION AND RACE

SOURCE: U.S. Department of Commerce, Bureau of the Census, *Statistical Abstracts of the United States 1978* (Washington: D.C.: Government Printing Office), p. 457 (adaptation).

__F__   4. Black and white people with 1 to 3 years of college make $20,000 a year.

__T__   5. Black and white people with 8 years of schooling make less money than persons with 4 years of high school.

Multiple-Choice Items

1. Which of the following statements is a statement of fact rather than opinion?

    1. Federal aid to local communities increases the national government.
  *2. The birth rate in the United States in the 1980s is increasing.
    3. America's involvement in the Vietnam War increased young people's distrust of government.
    4. Voting for Republicans is a vote to cut federal spending.

READ THE FOLLOWING STATEMENT AND RESPOND TO THE ITEM BELOW.

Sue: I am so tired of reading about criminals who are freed by the courts because the police did not interrogate them properly. Courts should not free guilty people because of technicalities. Suspects should be required to answer all the questions the police ask when they are apprehended.

Bill: I am not so sure I agree with you. After all, those "technicalities" during interrogation are designed to prevent police from obtaining forced confessions from people. Without rules governing interrogation procedures, what is to prevent the police from just grabbing anybody and forcing the person to confess to a crime?

---

2. Sue and Bill's dialogue indicates that they have a value conflict over

    1. individual guilt versus legal technicalities.
  *2. police power versus protection of the innocent.
    3. court procedures versus public safety.
    4. individual rights versus the right of police.

Essay Item

Write an essay that presents your solution to the current acid rain problem in the northeastern United States and southeastern Canada. Be sure to explain why your solution is more effective than previously proposed approaches.

Points for grading
- U.S. and Canadian government proposals are described (20 points).
- Industry proposals are mentioned (10 points).
- Student's proposal indicates a reasonable understanding of the problem with possible solution (20 points).

Sample test items were prepared by Stephen Rose, Price Laboratory School, University of Northern Iowa, Cedar Falls.

Bibliography

1. Adkins, D. C. *Test Construction: Development and Interpretation of Achievement Test.* Columbus, Ohio: Charles E. Merrill Publishing Co., 1974.

2. Bergman, J. *Understanding Educational Measurement and Evaluation.* Boston: Houghton Mifflin Co. 1981.

3. Bloom, B. S., and others. *Taxonomy of Educational Objectives: Handbook I, Cognitive Domain.* New York: David McKay, 1956.

4. Brown, F. G. *Measuring Classroom Achievement.* New York: Holt, Rinehart and Winston, 1981.

5. Denova, C. C. *Test Construction for Training Evaluation.* New York: Van Nostrand Reinhold Co., 1979.

6. Ebel, R. L. *Essentials of Educational Measurement.* Englewood Cliffs, N.J.: Prentice-Hall, 1979.

7. Erickson, R. C., and Wentling, T. L. *Measuring Student Growth: Techniques and Procedures for Occupational Education.* Boston: Allyn and Bacon, 1979.

8. Gronlund, N. E. *Constructing Achievement Tests.* Englewood Cliffs, N.J.: Prentice-Hall, 1976.

9. Ingram, C. F. *Fundamentals of Educational Assessment.* New York: Van Nostrand Reinhold Co., 1980.

10. Krathwohl, D. R., and others. *Taxonomy of Educational Objectives: Handbook II, Affective Domain.* New York: David McKay Co., 1964.

11. Kryspin, W. J., and Feldhusen, J. F. *Developing Classroom Tests: A Guide for Writing and Evaluating Test Items.* Minneapolis: Burgess Publishing Co., 1974.

12. Mager, R. F. *Preparing Instructional Objectives.* 2d ed. San Francisco: Fearon, 1975.

13. Nitko, A. J. *Educational Tests and Measurements: An Introduction.* New York: Harcourt Brace Jovanovich, 1983.

14. Popham, J. W. *Modern Educational Measurement.* Englewood Cliffs, N.J.: Prentice-Hall, 1981.

15. Schoer, L. A. *Test Construction: A Programmed Guide.* Boston: Allyn and Bacon, 1970.

16. Simpson, E. J. "The Classification of Educational Objectives in the Psychomotor Domain." *The Psychomotor Domain.* Vol. 3. Washington, D.C.: Gryphon House, 1972.

17. Steinmetz, J. E.; Romano, A. G.; and Patterson, M. M. "Statistical Programs for the Apple II Microcomputer." *Behavior Research Methods and Instrumentation,* 13 (Summer 1981): 702.

18. Swezey, R. W. *Individual Performance Assessment: An Approach to Criterion-Referenced Test Development.* Reston, Va: Reston Publishing Co., 1981.

19. Tchudi, Stephen N., and Yates, Joanne. *Teaching Writing in the Content Areas: Senior High School.* Washington, D.C.: National Education Association, 1983.

257

257006